HOCKEY'S STANLEY CUP FINALS

PERCY LEED

LERNER PUBLICATIONS ◆ MINNEAPOLIS

Lerner Publications Company
An imprint of Lerner Publishing Group, Inc.
241 First Avenue North
Minneapolis, MN 55401 USA

For reading levels and more information, look up this title at www.lernerbooks.com.

Main body text set in Mikado.
Typeface provided by HVD Fonts.

Library of Congress Cataloging-in-Publication Data

Names: Leed, Percy, 1968- author.
Title: Hockey's Stanley Cup Finals / Percy Leed.
Description: Minneapolis, MN : Lerner Publications, [2025] | Series: Lerner sports rookie. Championship games | Includes bibliographical references and index. | Audience: Ages 5–8 | Audience: Grades K–1 | Summary: "From slick shots to overcoming impossible odds, the Stanley Cup Finals has some of hockey's greatest moments. Young readers will enjoy learning more about what it is, its best players, and more"– Provided by publisher.
Identifiers: LCCN 2024008843 (print) | LCCN 2024008844 (ebook) | ISBN 9798765648018 (library binding) | ISBN 9798765661512 (paperback) | ISBN 9798765653913 (epub)
Subjects: LCSH: Stanley Cup (Hockey)—Juvenile literature. | National Hockey League—Juvenile literature. | Hockey—Juvenile literature.
Classification: LCC GV847.7 .L44 2025 (print) | LCC GV847.7 (ebook) | DDC 796.962—dc23/eng/20240307

LC record available at https://lccn.loc.gov/2024008843
LC ebook record available at https://lccn.loc.gov/2024008844

Manufactured in the United States of America
1-1010910-53362-6/4/2024

TABLE OF CONTENTS

CHAPTER 1
STANLEY CUP

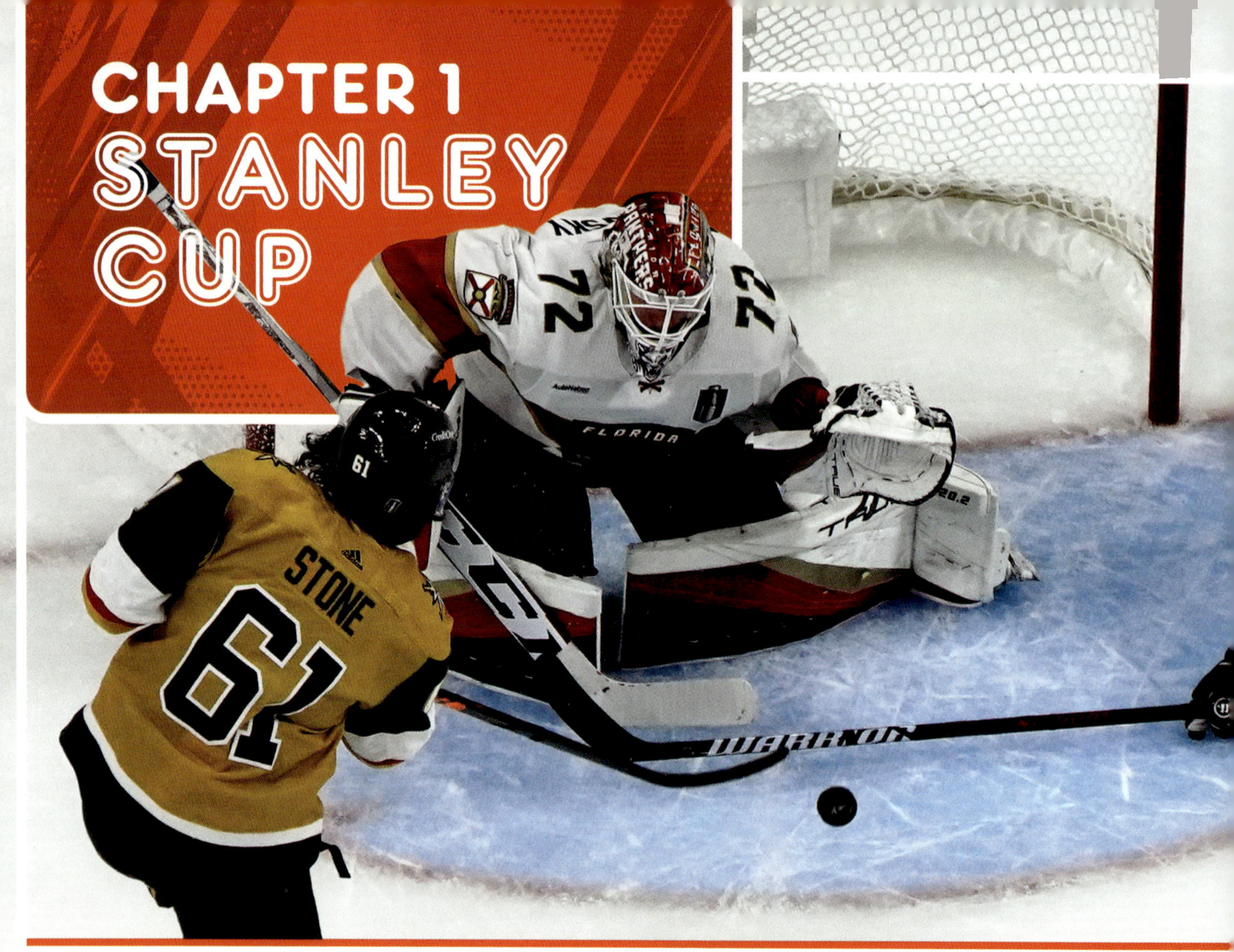

It was Game 5 of the 2023 Stanley Cup Finals. The Vegas Golden Knights kept scoring goals.

The Florida Panthers tried their best. But the game ended 9–3. The Golden Knights won their first Stanley Cup!

The Stanley Cup trophy has been around since 1892. The NHL formed in 1917. Since then, the Stanley Cup trophy has been awarded to the winner of the NHL.

CHAPTER 2
GREATEST MOMENTS

A thick fog covered the ice during Game 3 of the 1975 Finals. A Buffalo Sabres player shot the puck past the Philadelphia Flyers goalie.

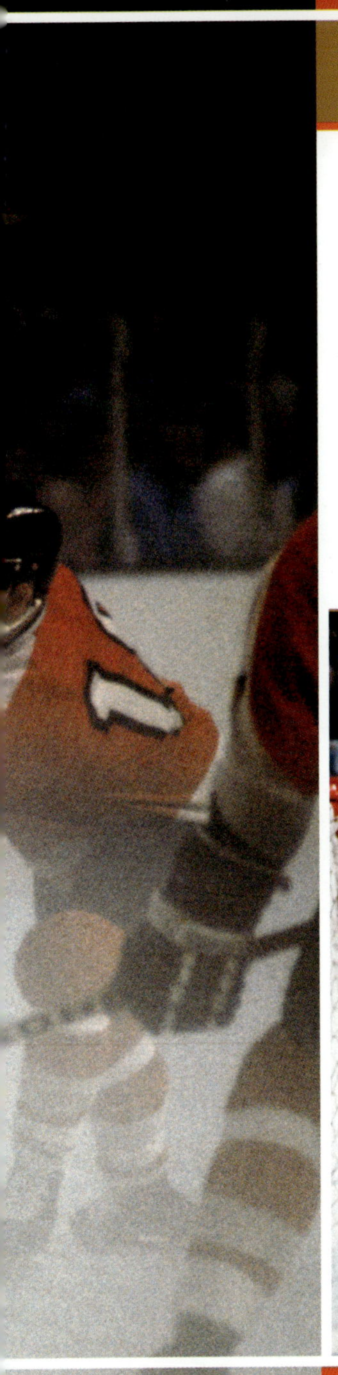

The fog was so thick the goalie couldn't see the puck until it was too late!

The New Jersey Devils were tied with the Dallas Stars in Game 6 of the 2000 Finals. Neither team would let the other score.

The game went into extra playing time twice. New Jersey took the shot. Goal! They won the Cup.

StubHub

The Vegas Golden Knights were a new team in 2018. Nobody thought they would make it very far. But they got all the way to the Finals in their first year in the NHL.

CHAPTER 3
BEST PLAYERS

Wayne Gretzky is one of the best hockey players of all time. He scored 18 goals in 31 Stanley Cup Finals games.

Saving goals is a hard job. But no goalie did it better than Patrick Roy. He won four Stanley Cups.

Pittsburgh Penguins star Sidney Crosby was 21 years old when he won his first Cup. His skills helped the Penguins win three Stanley Cups.

Nikita Kucherov went to the Stanley Cup Finals four times with the Tampa Bay Lightning. They won twice. He led the NHL in playoff scoring in 2020 and 2021.

CHAPTER 4
GAME NIGHT

Fans pack into crowded arenas on game night. Many wear their team's colors.

Excitement grows as famous singers perform before games.

Millions of people watch the games from home.

As soon as the puck drops, the players are off!

STANLEY CUP FINALS CHAMPS

Here are recent Stanley Cup winners!

2024 Florida Panthers

2023 Vegas Golden Knights

2022 Colorado Avalanche

2021 Tampa Bay Lightning

2020 Tampa Bay Lightning

2019 St. Louis Blues

2018 Washington Capitals

2017 Pittsburgh Penguins

2016 Pittsburgh Penguins

2015 Chicago Blackhawks

FUN FACTS

Each player from the winning team can spend a day with the Stanley Cup. They can take it almost anywhere, even on a roller coaster.

The NHL only had four teams in 1917. In 2023–2024, there were 32 teams.

In 2024, the Professional Women's Hockey League formed. Minnesota won the first Cup.

GLOSSARY

fog: a cloud close to the ground that makes it hard to see

NHL: National Hockey League

playoff: one of a series of games to decide a champion

LEARN MORE

Peters, Katie. *Hockey: A First Look.* Minneapolis: Lerner Publications, 2023.

Simons, Lisa M. Bolt. *Curious about Hockey.* Mankato, MN: Amicus, 2024.

Youssef, Jagger. *We Play Hockey!* New York: PowerKids, 2024.

INDEX

PHOTO ACKNOWLEDGMENTS

Image credits: AP Photo/John Locher, pp. 4–5, 7; John D. Hanlon/Sports Illustrated via Getty Images, pp. 8–9; Bruce Bennett Studios via Getty Images Studios/Getty Images, p. 9; David E. Klutho/Sports Illustrated via Getty Images, p. 10; B Bennett/Getty Images, p. 11; Jeff Bottari/NHLI via Getty Images, p. 12; Andrew D. Bernstein/Getty Images, p. 14; Focus on Sport/Getty Images, p. 15; AP Photo/Erin Hooley, p. 16; Dave Sandford/NHLI via Getty Images, p. 17; AP Photo/Lynne Sladky, pp. 18–19; Nathan Klima for The Boston Globe via Getty Images, p. 19; Peter Joneleit/Icon Sportswire via Getty Images, p. 21.

Design element: Winner Creative/Shutterstock. Cover: AP Photo/John Locher.